30 Minutes
... Before a
Presentation

Patrick Forsyth

KOGAN
PAGE

YOURS TO HAVE AND TO HOLD

BUT NOT TO COPY

First published in 1997

Kogan Page Limited
120 Pentonville Road
London N1 9JN

© Patrick Forsyth, 1997

British Library Cataloguing in Publication Data

A CIP record for this book is available from the British Library.

ISBN 0 7494 2359 5

Typeset by Saxon Graphics Ltd, Derby
Printed in England by Clays Ltd, St Ives plc

CONTENTS

The 30 Minutes Series

The Kogan Page 30 Minutes Series has been devised to give your confidence a boost when faced with tackling a new skill or challenge for the first time.

So the next time you're thrown in at the deep end and want to bring your skills up to scratch or pep up your career prospects, turn to the *30 Minutes Series* for help!

Titles available are:

30 Minutes Before Your Job Interview
30 Minutes Before a Meeting
30 Minutes Before a Presentation
30 Minutes to Boost Your Communication Skills
30 Minutes to Succeed in Business Writing
30 Minutes to Master the Internet
30 Minutes to Make the Right Decision
30 Minutes to Prepare a Job Application
30 Minutes to Write a Business Plan
30 Minutes to Write a Marketing Plan
30 Minutes to Write a Report
30 Minutes to Write Sales Letters

Available from all good booksellers.
For further information on the series, please contact:

Kogan Page, 120 Pentonville Road, London N1 9JN
Tel: 0171 278 0433 Fax: 0171 837 6348

INTRODUCTION

"The human brain starts working the moment
you are born and never stops until you stand up
to speak in public"

Sir George Jessel

Making a presentation might be called a career skill. It is
not only important as a task that forms part of an increas-
ing number of business jobs; it can also make a difference
to how you are perceived and even to how you get on in
your career.

I once asked a senior executive about the motivation level
of people who would be participating in a presentation skills
workshop I was to run for the organisation. He replied:
'They are all keen to attend – no one gets promoted in this
organisation unless they can make a good presentation.'
This is a common enough sentiment these days.

Yet presenting is not everyone's forte. For most people,
acquiring expertise in this area does not just happen. It

needs study and practice; it is, after all, a practical skill. Not everyone will be a great orator, but anyone can – and many must – turn in a workmanlike performance if they understand how to go about it.

The intention of this book is simple: to help the reader to be able to prepare, quickly and easily, and deliver a better presentation than might otherwise be possible. Above all, the aim is to ensure that the presentation will achieve its purpose. Reading this book will not remove the need for practice, but a sound understanding of the process can ensure that any practice helps to speed up the development of skills that make a positive difference to what is done 'on your feet'.

Patrick Forsyth
Touchstone Training and Consultancy
17 Clocktower Mews
London N1 7BB
Spring 1997

1

'UNACCUSTOMED AS I AM'

How do you feel if you know you have to make a presentation? Confident? Apprehensive? Terrified? If the answer is apprehensive or even terrified, relax – you are normal. Most people share your feelings to some extent.

In fact psychologists tell us that common feelings about presenting or public speaking are often almost wholly negative. The 'self-talk' we inflict on ourselves prior to having to speak in public consists of a catalogue of intimations of disaster. We say to ourselves such things as: 'I can't do it – I'm not ready'; 'the audience will hate it (or turn against me)'; 'I'll dry up'; 'I won't have sufficient material'; 'I don't know how to put it'; 'I'll lose my place'; and, at its most extreme, 'I'd rather die'.

If you stand up unprepared and ignorant of how to go about making your presentation, it may well be a disaster. But it need not be. With some knowledge, some practice and some forethought, there is no reason on earth why you should not make a good job of it. This book will tell you exactly how to go about it, but before turning to that, first consider the nature of presentations.

The importance of presentations

Presentations are important. There can be a great deal hanging on them – a decision, an agreement, a sale – and they can affect financial results and reputations too.

There are all sorts of reasons for making a presentation. You may have to speak:

- at an internal meeting
- externally, perhaps to distributors or customers
- to a committee (or board)
- at a conference or business event
- at social events from retirement parties to weddings.

You may have to speak to people you know, or to strangers; to more people senior to you in a work context; to difficult people; or to those who are much younger or older than you. You may need to speak to ten, 20 or 200 people, or even more.

All of these events and prospective audiences exhibit one common characteristic: they judge you by how you present. An example makes this clear. Imagine that you have to announce some policy change. Let us assume it is something eminently sensible which should be accepted without trouble. But start: 'Now ... um ... what I want to say is ... well, that is, basically ....' and you are well on the way to getting even the most innocuous message rejected.

It is a fact of life that something poorly presented can be poorly received regardless of the value of its content.

A significant opportunity

It is precisely because of this that presentations offer a real opportunity. If you can do them well (and you can) you will positively differentiate yourself from others who, from ignorance or lack of care, do an undistinguished or poor job.

It is worth quoting here a phrase used in a training film about making presentations, where a character describes presentations as being the 'business equivalent of an open goal'. Well put; this is not overstating the point and puts it in a memorable way. (I quote from the film *I wasn't prepared for that*, produced by Video Arts Limited. This is excellent, and I recommend seeing it to any reader wanting to augment their reading about the subject.

So, your motivation should not be in question here. There are few business skills it is more worthwhile to master than that of presentation: without it you not only feel exposed, you *are* exposed. The ground will not open up and allow you to disappear along with your embarrassment: rather, it is much more likely that there will be no agreement, no commitment, or an ominous message from the boss, saying: 'See me afterwards.'

Some degree of trepidation is understandable, but it can be either overcome or reduced to stop it overpowering your ability to work successfully. It may help to think of a balance: on one side there are things that can, unless dealt with, affect your ability to make a good presentation while on the other there are techniques that can assist the process. Paying the right kind of attention to both sides improves your capability.

Much of this book is about positive techniques. But let

us get the negative side out of the way first by looking at the possible difficulties, some of which are inherent to the process, and ways in which we can overcome them.

The hazards of communication

We communicate so much we tend to take it for granted, and regard much of it as easy. People may well say of a presentation that they know they could communicate the subject-matter perfectly well if they were talking to just one other person. But a moment's thought will remind you that communication is not easy; it can be downright difficult. How often in your organisation do communications misunderstandings, failures or derailments occur? How often do you hear people saying: 'What do you mean?'; 'I don't really understand'; 'If only you had said . . .'; 'But that's not what I meant'. How many times have you said such things yourself – or caused them to be said? (Be honest!)

The first rule here is easy. Ease of communication should never be taken for granted. It needs thought, care, and precision and this is doubly important when you present formally. With most presentations you only get one crack at it; it is not like a conversation which allows many opportunities for establishing understanding.

This means that every tiny detail matters. Presentations are inherently fragile. Small differences – an ill-chosen word or phrase, a hesitation, a misplaced emphasis – can all too easily dilute the impact.

At least communication problems are tangible and therefore easily tackled. If you resolve to take care your communication will be better and understanding more certain. You can work at getting this right. Many of the elements reviewed in this book assist this process. But what about other, less tangible, fears?

Presenters' nightmares

Workshop groups on presentations, when asked about their worries, usually produce a very similar list of factors. The top ten, in no particular order, are listed here with some suggestions for overcoming them:

1. Butterflies in the stomach. If you are nervous, you are likely to feel nervous. Without *some* apprehension, which can force you to focus on the job in hand, you would probably not do so well. Much of this feeling will fade as you get under way (and knowing this from practice helps), but you can help the process in a number of ways, for instance:

- take some deep breaths before you start (nerves tend to make you breathe more shallowly and starve you of oxygen), and remember to breathe as you go along (running out of breath to the point of gasping is a surprisingly common fault)
- take a sip of water just before you start
- do not eat a heavy meal before a presentation
- do not eat nothing (or rumbles may join the butterflies).

Alcohol (except possibly in extreme moderation) really does not help; at worst it may persuade you that you can do something you cannot and make matters worse as the truth dawns.

2. A dry mouth is easily cured. Never attempt to speak without a glass of water in front of you. Even if you do not touch it, knowing it is there is a comfort.

3. Not knowing what to do with your hands. The best solution is to give them something to do – hold the lectern or a pencil, make the occasional gesture – then forget about them. *Thinking* about them as you proceed will make matters worse.

4. Not knowing how loud to speak. Just imagine you are speaking to the farthest person in the room (if they were the only one there you would have little problem judging it), better still, try it beforehand.

5. A hostile reaction. The vast majority of groups want it to go well. They are disposed to be on your side. The only thing worse than standing on the platform knowing that you are not presenting well is being in the audience: think about it.

6. Not having sufficient material. This fear can be completely eradicated: if your presentation is well prepared (of which more anon), you will *know* there is the right amount.

7. Having too much material. As point 6; enough said for the moment.

8. Losing your place. Also tied in with preparation (and something else we will review in detail): your notes should be organised specifically so that it is unlikely that you will lose your place (and so that you can find it easily should you do so).

9. Drying up. Why should this happen? Dry mouth? Take a sip of water. Lose your place? Organise it so that this does not happen. Or just nerves? Well, some of the factors already mentioned will help; so too will preparation. And if it does happen, often it takes only a second to resume.

10. Misjudging the timing. This is something else speakers' notes can help with.

Many of these problems have a practical solution, something that removes or reduces the adverse effect. Thinking of it this way helps too. Try not to worry; it will be more likely to go well if you are sure it will and even more so if you are well organized.

Very few people can speak without forethought. It was Mark Twain who said, 'It usually takes me three weeks to prepare a good impromptu speech.' Preparation is the key to success and it is to that which we turn in the next chapter.

2

READY, GET SET . . .

Imagine that you have a presentation to make. The fact that you are reading this at all, means that you probably do. Few people will simply do nothing about it until the day and then just get up and speak. So what do you do? Addressing some of the dangers first will help us arrive at what is best practice here. What you might do is think of what you want to say first, then think of what follows – what you will say second, third and so on – and then write it down verbatim. Then, perhaps after some judicious amendment, you read it to your audience.

Wrong, wrong and wrong again.

This approach might sound logical, but it contains the seeds of disaster. We will pick up some alternative approaches as we continue. As it is a straightforward matter to address, let us take the reading issue first.

Do not try to read verbatim

Some people think, at least until they have more experience, that having every word down on paper and reading them out acts as a form of security. After all, what can go wrong if you have everything, right down to the last comma, in black and white in front of you? Well, two things in particular: first you will find that it is extremely difficult to read something smoothly, getting all the emphasis exactly where it needs to be, and do so fluently and without stumbling. The actors who record novels, and other books, as audio works deserve their pay cheques – real skill is involved here.

Most people speak very much better from notes which are an abbreviation of what they intend to say (we will return to just how much of an abbreviation and what you should have in front of you later). If you doubt this, just try it – read something out loud and see how it sounds. Better still, record it and *hear* how it sounds. In addition, certainly in a business context, you rarely need to be able to guarantee so exact a form of wording. It is usually more important to ensure that the emphasis, variety and pace is right and that is what is so difficult to achieve when reading.

Your audience

Good preparation starts with a clear view of your audience. First who are they? They may be people you know, men/women, expert or inexperienced about whatever topic you must address; there are many possible variations. The most important consideration, however, is the **audience's expectations**: what do they want?

Put yourself in their place. Facing a presentation, what do you say to yourself? Most people anticipate its impact on them: 'Will this be interesting, useful, long or short'; 'What will this person be like'?; 'Will I want to listen to them'; 'How will what they have to say help me?' Bearing audience viewpoint in mind is a major factor in ensuring a successful outcome.

Specifically, any audience *want* you to:

- 'know your stuff'
- look the part
- respect them, acknowledging their situation and their views
- discover links between what you say and what they want from the talk
- give an adequate message, so that they understand and can weigh up whether they agree with what is said or not (this is especially important if you are going to suggest or demand action of them)
- make it 'right for them' (for example, in terms of level of technicality)
- hold their attention and interest throughout.

It is equally important to bear in mind what audiences *do not want,* such as not being:

— confused
— blinded with science, technicalities or jargon
— lost in a convoluted structure (or with no structure at all)
— made to struggle to understand inappropriate language
— made to stretch to relate what is said to their own circumstances.

Nor do they want to listen to someone who, by being ill prepared, shows no respect for the group.

A good presenter will always have empathy with the audience; and this must be evident. Often this is something guided by prior knowledge but it can vary; you may need to speak to groups you do not know well. Always find out what you can and make use of everything you discover.

Successfully creating empathy requires an amalgam of various techniques we will explore individually later. Some relate to immediate practical factors that every presenter does well to remember. For example, I would not presume to tell you how to dress for a presentation, but it bears thinking about. Professionalism is, at least in part, inferred from appearance. Personal organisation too has a visual importance. You must not just be well organised, you must *look* well organised. Walking to the front, however confidently, is likely to be spoiled if you are clutching a bulging folder spilling papers.

Clear purpose

Rarely, if ever, will you be asked just to 'talk about' something. The most crucial question any intending presenter can ask themselves is simply:

- *Why is this presentation to be made?*

If you can answer that clearly, it will be easier both to prepare and present. Let us be clear here:

- *Objectives are not what you intend to say, they reflect what you intend to achieve.*

I regularly observe presentations (often carefully prepared) which are poor almost solely because they have no clear objectives. They rattle along reasonably well; but they do not *go* anywhere.

Objectives need not only to be clear, but must be spelt out in sufficient detail (certainly in your own mind and sometimes for others). They must be a genuine guide to what you will do. They also need to reflect not just what you want, but the audience's view too.

A much-quoted acronym provides a useful guide here:

SMART. This stands for:

Specific

Measurable

Achievable

Realistic, and

Timed.

As an example you might regard objectives linked to your reading of this book as:

- to enable you to ensure your future presentations come over in a way that audiences will see as appropriate and informative (*specific*)

- to ensure (*measurable*) action takes place afterwards (here you might link to any appropriate measure: from agreements or actions that group members take or commit to, to the volume of applause received!)

- to be right for you: sufficient, understandable, information in manageable form that will help you improve your future performance (an *achievable* result)

- to be *realistic* – hence a short book (if it took you several days to read the effort might prove greater than any benefit arising from it)

- and *timed;* a good factor to include in any objective. When are you going to finish reading this book? When is your next presentation? How far ahead of it should you prepare?

So, ask yourself whether you are clear in this respect before you even begin to prepare. If you know *why* the presentation must be made and *what* you intend to *achieve,* then you are well on the way to success. Time spent making sure you have a clear vision of what the objectives are is time well spent. It may only take a few moments. Or it may need more thought and take longer, but it is still worth doing and may save time on later stages of preparation.

With your purpose clear and a constant eye, as it were, on the audience, you can begin to assemble your message.

Deciding presentation content

There is more to this than simply banging down the points in sequence. A more systematic approach is essential; indeed, a more systematic approach can quickly become a habit of preparing in a way that guarantees results.

The following provides a full description of a tried and tested approach. This sets out the fullest degree of preparation necessary, but it is important to stress that this is not offered as a set of rules that must be followed slavishly. The important thing is to find, experiment with, refine and then use a method that suits *you*. In addition, practice and experience or other factors, such as familiarity with your chosen topic, may well allow you to adopt a 'shorthand' version of these approaches which is quicker, but still does the job.

Take one point at a time. Let us be clear of the way this aspect of presentation fits in with the route we will take beyond it.

First, a four-stage approach concentrates on helping sort out *what* you need to say (and what you should not say). Second, in a further stage, this is linked to ideas about speakers' notes; that is, what you can usefully have in front of you as you make the presentation, and here we investigate more about *how* you will put the message across; a final check is offered in the sixth stage. Then, in the next chapter, the structure that leads you through the presentation – the beginning, the middle and the ending –

investigates the techniques used to progress through the presentation, putting the emphasis where you want it to be. There is something of the chicken and egg here. Which comes first: preparation or structure. They are interrelated and both are vital, but the sequence chosen here works well and is intended to help the reader put a presentation together in a real life situation. (It might be useful to read on with an example in front of you and make some notes about how it can be developed as you go through.)

On to the detail of assembling the message.

Putting it together

It is not only essential to 'engage the brain before the mouth', but vital to think through – in advance – what a presentation must contain and, for that matter, not contain. This process of thinking through and preparation is recommended for its practicality and can be adapted to cope with any sort of presentation.

The stages are:

Stage 1: listing

Forget about everything such as sequence, structure and arrangement; just concentrate on and list – in short note (or keyword) form – every significant point that the presentation might usefully contain. Give yourself plenty of space (a larger sheet than the standard A4 is often useful: it lets you see everything at one glance). Set down the points as they occur to you, almost at random across the page. For something simple this might result only in a dozen words, or it might be far more.

You will find that this – akin to what some call 'mindmapping' – is a good thought prompter. It enables you to fill out the picture as one thought leads to another, with the freestyle approach removing the need to pause and try to link points or worry about sequence. With this done, and with some presentations it may only take a short time; you can move on to the second stage.

Stage 2: sorting

Now you can review what you have written down and begin to bring some order to it, deciding:

- what comes first, second and so on
- what logically links together, and how
- what provides evidence, example or illustration to the points.

At the same time, you can – and probably will - add extra things and have second thoughts about other items which you will delete. You need to bear in mind here the intended length of your presentation.

This stage can often be completed quickly by simply annotating and amending the first stage document. Using a second colour makes this quick and easy, as do link lines, arrows and anything that serves to enhance your original notes.

At the same time you can begin to add any more detailed elements that come to mind as you go through (including *how* you will present as well as *what* you will present). This can add, expand or amend your earlier notes, filling out the message and moving it nearer to final form.

Stage 3: arranging

Sometimes, by the end of stage 2, you will have notes that are sufficiently clear and from which you can work direct in preparing speaker's notes and finalising matters. If they could benefit from further clarification however, it may be worth rewriting them as a neat list. If you are using a computer, type your notes at this stage in preparation for printing them out in due course.

Rewriting is a useful opportunity for final revision. You should be left with a list which accurately reflects the content, emphasis, level of detail and so on that you feel is appropriate. You may well find you have to prune a bit to make things more manageable at this stage, rather than searching for more contents and additional points.

Stage 4: reviewing

This may be unnecessary. Sufficient thought may have been brought to bear through the earlier stages. However, for something particularly complex or important (or both) it may be worth running a final check. Sleep on it first perhaps, and avoid finalising matters too quickly – it may be difficult for you to be objective. After so much work, it is easy to find you cannot see the wood for the trees.

Make any final amendments to the list (if this is on screen it is a simple matter) and use this as your final 'route map' as preparation continues.

Stage 5: draft your speaker's notes

Now you can turn your firm intentions about content into something representing not only *what* will be said, but *how*. This must be done carefully, though your earlier work will help to make the process easier and quicker.

A couple of tips:

— if possible, *choose the right moment*. There are times when words flow more easily than others. It may help literally to talk it through out loud as you go through this stage. Interruptions can disrupt the flow and make the process take much longer, as you recap and restart again and again. Choosing the right moment and ensuring that you have uninterrupted time in a comfortable environment will all help

—*keep going*. Do not pause and agonise over a phrase, heading or some other detail. You can always come back to it; indeed, it may be easier to complete later. If you keep going you maintain the flow, allowing consistent thinking to carry you through the structure to the end so that you can 'see' the overall shape of the presentation. Once you have the main detail down then you can go back and fine tune, adding any final thoughts to complete the picture. Choosing the right format for your notes can be very helpful; something we will investigate in a moment.

Stage 6: a final check

A final look (perhaps after a break) is always valuable. This is also the time to consider rehearsal. Talk it through to yourself, to a tape recorder or a friend or colleague, or go through a full scale dress rehearsal.

> *Note:* If you are speaking as part of a team, *always* make sure that the speakers get together ahead of the event to rehearse, or at least discuss, any possible overlaps *and* the handovers. You should be aiming for what will appear to the group to be a seamless transition between the separate contributors.

Thereafter, depending on the nature of the presentation, it may be useful to spend more time either revising or just reading over what you plan to do. However, you should not overdo the revision at this stage; there comes a time to be satisfied that you have it right and stick with it.

Every stage of this preparation process is vital and should not be skimped. Preparation does get easier however. You will find that, with practice, you will begin to produce material that needs less amendment and that getting it down in the first place and the subsequent revision begin to take less time.

At the end of the day, as has been said already, you will need to find your own version of the procedures set out here. A systematic approach helps, but the intention is not to over-engineer the process. What matters is that you are comfortable with your chosen approach, that it works for you. If this is the case then, provided you never lose sight of the purpose of the presentation, it will become a habit requiring less and less conscious thought, yet still guaranteeing that you turn out something which you are content meets the needs of the particular occasion – whatever they may be.

So far so good. With a clear idea of what you want to say, we can add some thoughts about the form and style of what you will need in front of you to guide you on the day.

Speaker's notes

For most people, having *something* in front of them is essential. The question is, what exactly should it be? Speaker's notes have several roles:

- to boost confidence: in the event you may not need your notes, but knowing they are there is useful in itself

- to act as a guide to what you will say and what order you will say it in

- to assist you to say it in the best possible way by producing the right variety, pace, emphasis, etc, as you go along.

On the other hand it must not act as a straitjacket, stifling flexibility and spontaneity. After all, what happens if your audience's interest suggests that you digress or provide them with more detail before proceeding? Or the reverse: you may want to recast or abbreviate something you plan to say? Or if, as you get up to speak for half an hour the person in the chair whispers, 'Can you keep it to 20 minutes? We are running a bit behind.' Good notes should help you cope with these and other scenarios as well.

Set out below are some tried and tested approaches, but the intention is not to suggest that you follow them slavishly. It is important to find what suits you, so you may want to try some of the approaches mentioned, but amend or tailor them to suit your kind of presentation as exactly as possible.

One point is worth making at the outset: it is advantageous to adopt (even if not straightaway) a consistent approach to how you work here. You are likely to become quicker at getting your preparation done if you do so, and a successful outcome is all the more likely.

The following might be adopted as **rules**:

- Legibility is essential (you must use sufficiently large type or writing, avoid adding tiny, untidy embellishments and remember that notes must be suitable to be used standing up and therefore at a greater distance from your eyes than if you sat to read them)

- The materials must be chosen carefully to suit your purposes. Some people favour small cards, others larger sheets. A standard A4 ring binder works well (one with a pocket at the front may be useful to carry items you want with you). Whatever you choose, make sure it *lies flat*; it is certain to be disconcerting if a folded page turns back – especially if you repeat a whole section, as

I once saw happen (I can still vividly remember the moment when the speaker realised what was happening – sheer Schadenfreude I'm sorry to say!)

- Use one side only of the paper. This allows amendment and addition if necessary and makes the total package easier to follow

- Always number the pages of your material (yes, one day, as sure as the sun rises in the morning, you will drop it). Some like to number in reverse order, which gives some idea as to how much time remains until the end

- Separate different types of note: for example, regarding *what* you intend to say and *how* (that is, emphasis, etc)

- Use colour and symbols to help you find your way, yet minimise what must be noted.

At this point an example will help. On the next few pages the text of the start of a presentation about time management is set out, leading into a short review of how time might be best managed. The parallel page shows what might usefully be in front of the presenter during this session. The first is pretty much verbatim. The second is an example of the quantity and style of guidance you might adopt.

Example: presentation (the first part of a short talk on time management)

'Good morning. Let's get straight down to business; as you might guess this is one session that should make a point of starting on time! Indeed, time management is important to everyone.

I am sure we are all busy. Some of us may occasionally feel we have more to do than we can reasonably be expected to cope with – or perhaps regularly would be a better word. We may also feel that some of the things we are not getting to are more important, or more interesting, than the jobs bogging us down. And, as one harassed person said to me only a few days ago, *'I would just like a moment to think'*. It all matters. We will not be effective if everything is always done in a head-long rush.

Today, I want to suggest that we *can* create more time. Who would like five extra minutes? That may not seem much, hardly time to pour a cup of tea much less do anything useful, but if we save even that *every working day* it is 18 hours in a year – and which of us could not put to good use what amounts to nearly two whole extra days!

Time is a resource, and today I want to help us think about how to maximise its use.

So much time is wasted. Interruptions, unnecessary telephone conversations, seemingly interminable meetings – need I go on? We all know the feeling. What can we do about it? Well, there's good news and bad news.

The bad news is that good time management is difficult, and pressure makes it more so; certainly, getting it right needs conscious effort. But many of the things that

Example: Speaker's notes

Intro:	start on time!	1

	⬤ Busy – too much
	        – routine versus important
	   "time to think"
	   – not effective	

	⬤ (today) <u>create</u> time	example: 5 mins? 5 mins × 220 = c. 18 hours more than 2 days!
(S1)	TIME IS A RESOURCE	
	but	

	⬤ So much waste – interruptions
	             – telephone
	             – <u>meetings!</u>	

	So? Bad/good news	
	⬤ Bad – difficult + pressure	
	⬤ Good – attitude – techniques ──────▶	<u>result</u> – organised – priorities – avoid waste – manage
Where time goes now	work pattern (then techniques to improve)	
TIME:		

> make it work are common sense, and good habits can be acquired surprisingly quickly.
>
> So, the good news is that with the right attitude, and with diligent use of some well-applied techniques we can make a difference – be organised, focus on the priorities, avoid wasting time and manage the interruptions in a way that minimises them.
>
> Let's look at where time goes *now*, then at some of the techniques involved in keeping our work pattern under control . . .'

The detail on the speaker's notes needs to be just sufficient for a well-prepared speaker to be able to work from it comfortably. Consider the devices this example uses, and try to bear in mind as you do so the effect that the use of a second (or even third) colour – which cannot be reproduced here – would have on its ease of use. The grey tint represents a highlighting pen. This would be more dramatic in fluorescent yellow, but its utility can still be shown clearly in black and white print.

Back to the ideas incorporated. There should be things here you can copy or adapt, or which prompt additional ideas that suit you. Used on the example page are:

- **Main divisions.** The page – imagine it is A4 – is divided (a coloured line is best) into smaller segments, each creating a manageable area on which the eye can focus with ease; this helps to ensure that you do not lose your place

- **Symbols,** which save space and visually jump off the page, making sure you do not miss them. It is best to avoid possible confusion by always using the same symbol to represent the same thing – and maybe also to restrict the overall number used; too many might make the notes too difficult to follow

- **Columns.** These separate different elements of the notes. There are various options here in terms of the number of columns you choose and what goes where

- **Space.** Turning over takes only a second (often you can end a page where a slight pause is necessary anyway); it is always best to give yourself plenty of space, not least to facilitate amendments and, of course, to allow individual elements to stand out

- **Emphasis.** This must be as clear as content; again, a second colour helps

- **Timing.** An indication of time elapsed (or still to go) can be included, as often as you find useful; remember the audience love to have time commitments kept

- **Options.** These can be particularly useful as a separate element. Options can be added or omitted depending on such factors as time and feedback. They help to fine-tune the final delivery and are good for confidence also.

- Finally here, as recommended earlier, there is clear **page numbering**.

Good preparation and good notes go together. If you are well prepared, confident of your material and confident also that you have a really clear guide in front of you, you are well on the way to making a good presentation.

Rehearsal

Preparation may be defined as including rehearsal, but they are different things. At one end of the scale is just talking it through in your head (not least to check duration). At the other is getting one (or more) people to listen to a dry run – though, of course, you should aim to make it not too dry. You can go further, for example, using a video recorder or organising a more formal counselling session. The choice is yours and should be dictated by the importance and nature of the event and the confidence you have in what you can and will do.

Rehearsal can, if possible, also sensibly include such things as:

- checking out the speaking area
- trying out slides (and equipment)
- ensuring a clear brief from anyone who will be in the chair. It is annoying to be interrupted as the chair invites the group to go take a coffee break, when you were only planning to speak for perhaps two more minutes. Having to negotiate such things during the presentation will destroy the flow.

Final rules

Throughout the process of preparation always remember to:

- think positive (actively combating that all too common negative 'self talk')
- give preparation *sufficient* time (which includes starting it early enough and, which is sometimes more difficult, organising that time without interruption).

Ready, steady, go is always the best order. In the next chapter we move on to the presenter's equivalent of go – putting it over.

3

GO – MAKING THE PRESENTATION

Making the presentation incorporates *what* you must do, and *how* you do it. Again, to keep matters manageable we will look first at what you might call the 'mechanics' of how you structure and move through a presentation and then in the next chapter at some tricks of the trade that can make presenting easier for you to do and enliven it further for the audience. Keeping an eye on what the audience expects has been mentioned; this continues to be important throughout the process.

Signposting

This is a technique that can help you and your audience alike. Signposting, or labelling, does just what it says: it points out what is coming. People like to have an overview and they like to know where they are. Helping them in this respect scores points and makes an audience

feel comfortable both with themselves and with the presenter. They stop asking themselves 'Where is this going?'
and instead say 'Right, sounds as if it makes sense, what
comes next?': and they will listen.

The next few lines contain another example of a man-
ager who is introducing a project review meeting with a
short presentation:

> Let's be sure we are all clear what we need to
> do in the next hour or so. I intend to bring us up
> to speed on progress to date, then call for sec-
> tion heads to add any comments about their
> respective areas, then we need to see what new
> actions are necessary to keep us in line to hit
> the deadline and what must be done before the
> next meeting.

Again, this is an overall statement. It might be followed by
more signposting as the first part of what was indicated
actually began:

> Right, let's get up to date. I will comment about
> what stage we have reached first, then about
> how costs are working out, then about feedback
> that may mean some fine tuning.

And this, in turn, might be followed by more, at the next
level down:

> Turning to costs, we need to think about materials
> and staff separately. I will start with materials . . .

Even this level might need subdividing. It really is true to
say that you cannot overuse signposting (though it could
usefully be a little more spaced out than in the example
above!).

The value of this technique in terms of keeping things organised is obvious. Further, it is likely to be more useful with long and complex presentations than when speaking for five minutes on one straightforward topic – though that is not to say that any presentation can afford to be disorganised.

In addition, signposting can be used in various ways, not only with structure but to flag individual elements, that is, *what is coming*. For example:

- *Here's an example of how that works* (stating specifically that an example is coming)
- *For instance, . . .* (implying that an example is coming)
- *Now, if we look at some figures carefully, it will make a good example of . . .* (as well as drawing attention to the coming example, emphasising the need to pay attention to detail)

It may also be useful sometimes to signpost *the nature of what is coming*. For example:

- *Let me digress for a moment* (making it clear the next thing said will be aside from the main – and perhaps identified – content)
- *Perhaps I can add something here* (the digression is extra to the original content)
- *On a less serious note* (implying an aside that may amuse).

In using this sort of device you may add to its value if you explain the *why* of the matter also: 'Here's an example that will link what I've been saying to your day-to-day work'.

All this does more than just inform; it also influences. Your choice of words can prompt an audience to pay particular attention, relate what is being said to their situation, make a note, remember something that needs to be kept in mind alongside what comes next and so on.

But we are getting ahead of ourselves so, to use a specific signpost of my own, we turn now from indicating structure to the structure itself.

In the beginning . . .

It is said that you never get a second chance to make a good first impression. It may be a cliché, but ignore it at your peril. A good start has a positive effect on the audience and on the presenter – it can be a wonderful feeling when, after your initial apprehension, you realise you are a couple of minutes in and all is going well; it boosts your confidence, helping you successfully deliver what is still to come.

It follows logically that the beginning needs especially careful preparation. Notes for this stage may need to be just a little fuller than elsewhere, especially when you consider the complexity of what you are trying to do in the opening.

The beginning is an introduction. It must be clear *why* the presentation is being made (remember what was said about objectives in Chapter 2). The scene must be set, the topic introduced and the theme stated (and, possibly, boundaries drawn – 'In the time available, I will highlight what seem to me the key issues . . .'). All this must be done clearly and, at the same time, you must aim to have some impact on the audience in two different ways:

- getting their attention and interest
- establishing an appropriate rapport with them.

Getting the audience's attention

There are two broad ways of starting:
- with the formalities

■ with something ahead of the formalities.

'Good morning, ladies and gentlemen, thank you for the opportunity to talk to you today about presentation skills . . .' may be suitable on some occasions. As long as this element is brief it is seen as a formality and the audience will go along with it expecting something more interesting to be along soon.

The formalities may be important. If a 'thank you' is called for, for instance, I am certainly not saying it should be omitted, but it does not have to take precedence. For example, try something like:

> 'The next thirty minutes will help you do an important job better and more quickly than you do it now; what job? – making presentations. Before saying something about how you can be more effective in this task, let me thank . . .'

Often the second approach may have more impact.

That said, you may find it useful to think of ways in which you can aim to get people's attention. You may be able to add to it, but the following list starts the process:

■ *Surprise them with something they do not know*: 'Hot off the presses – the trade journal feature we have been waiting for is out and it gives us a real plug, this will . . .'

■ *Ask them a question*: 'How many hours of productivity were wasted last month?' (This can be rhetorical and closely followed by 'Let me tell you, it was . . .' or actual, though the latter can lead to early digression if the response is not quite as expected.)

■ *Trigger their curiosity*: 'How many of you are afraid of spiders?' In a talk on public speaking this may appear an odd beginning, but it prompts active response – people ask themselves - 'How does this fit in?' Then, if a link is quickly made with other fears including that of speaking in public, you can continue with their full attention (at least for the moment)

- *Remind them of something, such as a common experience:* 'This time last year, when we met at last year's annual planning meeting, I said . . .'

- *Give them something to watch:* 'Time is running out . . .' could be accompanied by a gesture, perhaps slowly taking off your watch (which may, in any case be more use in front of you) or pointing to a wall clock

- *Say something designed to be dramatic and say it in a dramatic way:* 'The next half hour can change the organisation's fortunes forever. How? By . . .'

- *Tell them an anecdote, perhaps with a humorous edge – but be careful (see page 55):* 'Once upon a time . . .'

- *Apprise them of a fact which is relevant to the topic:* '90 per cent of the telephone support staff are asking for leave in the first part of July, and that is just one reason for reviewing certain staffing policies . . .'

- *Quote something, preferably something relevant, that makes a point:* 'The physicist Neils Bohr said "Prediction is always difficult, especially of the future". He had a point. But I must try and do just that.'

- *Say nothing:* Well, say something, but then pause. 'Listen (*presenter counts ten silently*). Not a sound – isn't *anyone* doing any work around here?'

Such devices can be linked, adapted or added to, but the first few words – or sometimes few sentences – must always actively seek attention. They may sometimes usefully be linked to some clear signposting of what is to come thereafter.

Creating rapport with the audience

No one wants to sit through a presentation that is tedious, dull and irrelevant. But even a speaker's 'self talk' is largely negative, it is probably true to say that the audience have primarily positive feelings. They *want* it to be interesting and successful. They tend to give the speaker the benefit of the doubt and if they warm to you as well as to what you say, this increases the likelihood of overall acceptance.

So there is a need to foster group feeling and this means you must have a clear idea of how you want to be regarded. Do you want to be seen as expert, authoritative, sympathetic – or what? Such attributes are not, of course, mutually exclusive and you must match your projection to the occasion and the audience.

The power of enthusiasm

One factor is universally useful – enthusiasm. It is one of the few good things in life that is contagious. It can have a powerful effect. Expressing it – so long as it is sincere – tends to make you appear more animated, which is obviously a good thing, and it also establishes the flavour of your presentation. Even a funeral tribute may need some degree of enthusiasm – it should be a standard part of your approach.

Beyond this, there are various other factors that, together or separately, can assist in building your rapport with the audience. For example:

- *Select the appropriate form of address*. Consider the difference between the following:

  — *We should consider . . .*

  — *You should consider . . .*

  — *I think you should consider . . .*

  — *Most people find . . . worth considering*

all of which have a different feel to them. Other phraseology affects feeling in similar ways, for example, the difference between *must do . . .; should do . . .; might find it useful to . . .,* etc. Choice here indicates your approach, which people can then form a view of

- *Use a compliment.* Do not overdo it and sound patronising, but something like 'Being expert in this area yourselves you will . . .' can be useful

- *Link your situation or experience to theirs:* Use phrases like 'We all know the problem of . . .', which make it clear you are part of the group rather than standing outside *talking at it.*

The beginning is, by definition, brief and must be regarded, and organised, as a suitable proportion of the whole. It must have its own separate entity, yet allow a smooth transition into the middle, the meat, of the presentation.

Before it does so, however, it must achieve the tasks you have set out for it and engender the right response in the audience. Both are worth a word or two before we move on.

Your tasks for the beginning

The main tasks you have to undertake will probably include:

- defining and describing the topic
- spelling out the objectives
- explaining why this is sensible or necessary
- describing something of the structure
- beginning with something in a way that catches interest and raises audience expectations that what follows will be something they will want to hear

- beginning, if possible, to link to satisfying their specific expectations
- establishing a feeling that the presentation is of relevance – *to them*.

All these will usually be appropriate. You may also need to achieve things that are more specific to particular occasions: encouraging people to keep an open mind, setting the scene for later participation, or making clear something like the level of technicality or depth you intend to go into or the point, in terms of experience or background, from which you are starting.

The audience response you intend to generate

It is also useful to think about the feelings the audience would express if quizzed at each point as you move from the beginning to the middle. Would they feel that:

- it is accurately directed at them?
- their specific needs are being borne in mind?
- the speaker is engaging, or at least worth listening to?
- they are starting to identify (and agree with) what is said?

If so, you can move on with confidence and use a good start as a solid foundation on which to build.

A final point worth mentioning concerns **administrative matters.** It may be important to welcome specific people, notify them of a break or refreshment arrangement if it is a long session, or tell them the policy regarding smoking, for example. The question then is when to do this so that it does not dilute the effectiveness of the start (it is not, one hopes, the most striking thing you will say).

There is no reason why a presentation cannot have two starts; something that was hinted at earlier. Begin – with some impact – quickly digress to deal with administrative matters; then restart, treating the restart as the real beginning. This is partly a matter of taste, but it is worth considering.

One administrative point no one minds hearing about concerns *duration*. It is slightly uncomfortable to sit and listen with no idea how long something is expected to last: ten minutes, 20, an hour, two? So this can be usefully mentioned: 'I promise few things for the next hour, but one thing I do promise is to finish on time. You will be out of here by 12 noon.'

The heart of the matter: the middle

Here is the core, where the need for good organisation and structure is greatest. This is the longest part of the presentation and it is here you must:

- put across the detail of your message
- maintain attention and develop interest

and execute the task in a way that continues to focus on the audience and reflect their needs and situation.

Structure is key

Some presenters have what one might call an 'and another thing' style. They move from one thing to another and, although separate points are identified, there is no real clue as to the rhyme or reason of it all. Any structure that may exist is buried under the push from 'and now, . . . ' to 'and next . . .'.

The rules here are clear:

- You must originate a clear structure and keep it firmly in mind throughout
- If necessary, you must explain the logic 'I am taking things in this order so that . . .'

- You must spell out early on what your chosen structure is (in whatever degree of detail is appropriate)
- You must keep people posted throughout by regular signposting
- You must link appropriately to any visual aids (or hand-outs).

All these allow the audience to keep things in context as the message builds up, preventing you rambling and thus being difficult to follow.

The job here is to move from point to point in a way that does each one justice, maintains continuity and creates a clear overall message. On the other hand, the intention is not to create too much rigidity. You need to maintain some flexibility yourself, and may want to retain the ability to surprise the group by not spelling out everything that is to come.

There are still a number of points to consider if everything is to be got over as you wish; so (more signposting) now some key 'dos' and 'don'ts':

What to do

- *Always be clear*. Communication is inherently difficult in the sense that there are plenty of possibilities for misunderstanding. The responsibility lies with you. You have to make things clear. It is no good thinking 'what's the matter with these people? Are they all idiots?' when the truth is that it is you who is being vague or obtuse.

So actively seek to be clear, and remember that it makes an excellent impression if people expect something to be complicated and then find it is easier than they thought. And worry about the little things as much as the big. If you have significant complexities to go through you will be

41

inclined to concentrate on them, but be careful not to let drop a phrase which, through lack of thought, and thus precision, dilutes understanding.

■ *Maintain the audience focus*: this point has been made already, but stands repetition as it is vital to be seen to be directing what you do accurately in light of the circumstances of the people in the group

■ *Be descriptive*: presentations should paint a picture. This can be done in various ways. By simile – 'It is like . . .' – the better the allusion chosen the more powerful the point

■ *Be memorable*: not in every word you say, which would be an impossible task. But using some especially apt or telling phrase can be powerful (you can repeat it too: try using it, for example, as part of your signposting)

■ *Use visual aids*: these may be in the form of slides or may be more in the nature of exhibits (eg product samples), but they can be important. They add variety, focus the message and assist description, sometimes dramatically; we all know the way a graph, for instance, can put over a point in a moment that would take much longer to explain verbally. More of visual aids in Chapter 5

■ *Use your physical manner to augment your message*: enthusiasm is part of this. So are gestures and animation, and we will return to both in more detail. There are many ways of letting your intentions show

■ *Offer proof where necessary*: if you seek agreement from people (not always the case) remember you cannot simply set out the facts as you see them. If you say 'It is a very practical solution', the audience response may well be 'Well he would say that wouldn't he?' Adding other opinions, using references, test or research results, or whatever suits your case, will strengthen your argument*

- *Use your voice*: this is obviously your greatest asset in presenting. Variety, pace and emphasis are all essential and these elements (along with others) can continuously strengthen your presentational power (see page 53).

- *Use, and show, a 'master plan'*: if there is particular complexity or need for clarity it may be worth having one overall visual aid (a slide or flipchart sheet, perhaps) that acts as the 'contents page' for your presentation. This can be reshown and used to punctuate the proceedings, acting to recap, look ahead, ensure things remain in context and to lead on to the next point.

What not to do

Conversely, there are a number of things to watch out for and avoid. These include no:

- *Unnecessary verbal padding*: here I am thinking not so much of simply rambling (which is to be avoided) but of words and phrases such as the ubiquitous 'basically' (at the start of every other sentence it is incorrect and annoying); phrases like 'at this moment in time' (when 'now' will do nicely) – doubtless you can think of more

- *Overuse of jargon*: sometimes described as professional shorthand, it can be useful – why say four words if you can replace them with a set of initials, for instance? But, it only works when it is understood by everybody – otherwise it confuses and dilutes meaning. Using

---

* If your presentations habitually need to be persuasive, then it may be worth checking out the skills involved; see, for instance, my book *Agreed! Making Management Communication More Persuasive* Kogan Page (1993).

inappropriate jargon is also regarded as a lack of courtesy and respect for the group

- *Vague or bland terminology*: what does it mean to say something is 'quite nice', 'rather large' or 'very good'? It might be sufficient if the point was minor, but if a different kind of description – a *more powerful* kind of description – would do the job better, avoid it

- *Unwarranted assumptions*: about anything to do with the audience that you do not truly know accurately. For example, do not make assumptions about their level of knowledge, experience, views, fears, prejudices – whatever. Predicating what you say on something they know to be false hardly increases your impact; even more so when people believe you *should* have known the facts of the matter.

Following all these rules and the use of the various techniques reviewed as we proceed can ensure that you move smoothly through the main segment of your presentation. It can ensure that people are happy, or at least content, to follow your progress. It means that you are well on the way to achieving your aims. But there is one other thing that needs doing if you are to stay on track.

Watch for and use feedback

Even when you are not seeking participation any group will provide signs to guide you and, if you are quick on your feet, to enable you to fine tune what you still have to do.

Keep an eye out and listen for any hints about how the audience is reacting:

- Are they fidgeting or restless?
- Are they nodding or whispering together?

- Can you ask for feedback (with a quick question and perhaps a show of hands)?
- Can you anticipate objection and snuff it out fast? ('I'll bet you're thinking this is just too complicated. Seems that way, but let me show you how . . .').

Some observations obviously indicate positive feedback, others may need double checking: a whispered comment to a neighbour may be 'that's a good point' or 'did you watch TV last night?' Others still may be obviously negative, but provide useful feedback allowing you to duck incoming missiles! As Bob Hope once said of his early days, 'If the audience liked you, they didn't applaud – they just let you live.'

The reassurance provided by positive feedback is likely to boost confidence, and if some adjustment is necessary then the options element recommended in the earlier discussion of speakers' notes is a useful starting point for what needs to be done 'on the run'.

A happy ending

There is satisfaction in a happy ending. Threads come together, conclusions are reached and everything is generally wrapped up satisfactorily. The end of a presentation, like the beginning, is important: disproportionately important. Like the beginning it may need special thought in preparation to get it right.

The intentions are clear:

- to make any final points and summarise
- to meet the brief (drawing conclusions, making a recommendation; whatever is necessary)
- to end on a positive and if possible a high note
- overall, to finish up a presentation that is felt to have achieved its objectives for its audience.

So, first decide what the end point is. Your objectives, and the logic and structure of what you have been going through, will usually lead naturally to an end point. There is a significant opportunity here. Summarising effectively is not the easiest thing to do. Because not everyone finds it easy, it impresses when it is well done. It is worth effort to create this impression.

It can be easy to spoil a good ending. So first, some 'don'ts':

- **Do not** – seem to end yet continue on (and sometimes on), saying 'finally' three times and *still* rambling on to some new digression
- **Do not** – rush for the end (perhaps because time is running out or from sheer relief) and let it become disjointed and confused
- **Do not** – repeat points inappropriately; summary means exactly that and is not an excuse to revisit half the presentation again
- **Do not** make the last thing you say 'thank you'. Even if there is a powerful conclusion finishing with 'Thank you very much for the opportunity, I am grateful for your time and . . .', sounds ineffectual and inconclusive.

Of course, I am not suggesting that you omit a thank you when it is called for, only that you do not place it last. An approach more like the following: 'Well, I am grateful for your time. Thank you for listening. I will end with one final thought . . .' may suit better.

A sign off phrase

This element of your presentation may dwell in the minds of the audience longer than most of the other things you say, so it should be appropriate and well chosen, and even, on occasion, memorable.

The techniques here are very like the list offered in discussing the beginning – a question or a quotation, for example, may be joined by an injunction to act.

Timing

The key to successful comedy, it is said, is timing. It is important in presenting too. And at the end, the rule is simple: **always finish on time**. Good timekeeping means disciplining yourself, but it is a courtesy and, perhaps even more important, it impresses. Start by saying '. . . and in the half hour I have . . .', and include near the finish '. . . I see my time is almost up, so . . .' and you will gain additional respect. You also avoid the very real hazard of people starting to think about the time – 'Five minutes over already, I wonder how much longer . . .' – which always acts as a distraction.

Sometimes, however, things conspire to handicap your ability to keep to time.

The unforeseen

All sorts of things can happen along the way to create interruptions. Anticipate them and they will not surprise and so distract you. And – another rule – *never compete with an interruption*. If someone comes into the room with coffee on a trolley and begins to make a noise, acknowledge it and deal with it. People will think it odd if you pretend not to be distracted and plough on regardless.

At a more formal occasion, involve the chair – 'Do you want me to pause for a moment?' They may then put a stop to the interruption, or agree to a momentary break.

Audience control is also important. If you are the sole presenter and there is no Chair, you effectively take on that role and can decide how things like questions will be dealt with. For example, they can be held until the right moment or dealt with after the formal proceedings have finished (on time).

And that, as they say, is all there is to it. Well – perhaps not quite. There is more to come. Actually quite a bit more, all of which has to be borne in mind, and all of which can influence the final outcome and help make your presentations successful.

So, let us end this chapter with an analogy. Can you drive a car? Do you remember learning to drive? (Imagine, if you do not drive, some similarly complex skill.) You doubtless recall a stage when you were convinced that driving was a physical impossibility.

If you were like me, you went through a stage of being convinced that the innumerable things that had to be done simultaneously – steering, changing gear, watching the road, indicating (and thinking, for goodness sake!) – were simply too much for you and that you would never be able to drive. But eventually it all came together and, while driving always demands concentration, for the experienced driver some aspects of it become second nature. It really is possible and everything necessary really can all happen at once.

Presenting is similar in many ways. There is a good deal not only to think about but to do, and to do seemingly simultaneously. Let me assure the less experienced reader in particular that practice really does ensure that the techniques involved here will come together, just like the seemingly disparate skills involved in learning to drive. A sound knowledge of what is involved is the first step to pulling it all together.

I said there was more to come, and there is. In the next chapter we look at a variety of ways in which power and precision can be added to what a presenter does.

TECHNIQUES FOR ADDING POWER AND PRECISION

A well-prepared and well-structured presentation is essential, but more than that is necessary if you are to inject a real spark of life. The maxims make it sound very simple: stand up, look them in the eye, and let them have it. However, there is a significant number of details that should be borne in mind if you want to add to what might otherwise be a serviceable but routine presentation.

In view of the number I had better start by following some of my own strictures, and lay down some signposting. Following the short maxims above there are four main topics to consider, and they are:

- Footwork
- Eyes
- Hands, arms and gestures
- Voice.

One other matter is also dealt with in this chapter, and that is the use of humour; an appropriate note on which to end the list, perhaps.

Feet firmly on the floor

Feet may seem like a minor detail, but your footwork influences your stance and hence your style, and it can keep you comfortable – or otherwise.

First, consider *where* you stand. There is a variety of options you can choose or which may be chosen for you if you have not organised the environment yourself. Whether you are on a conference platform, behind a lectern (or simply a table), or in front of a formal position at a table, for instance inside a U-shaped layout, all present slightly different problems and opportunities. There is more security behind a table with a lectern to hold on to, but there may be more rapport with a group if you are located among them. Each situation requires different organisation. For instance, a clipboard that you can carry with you if necessary works better than a fistful of loose papers if you have no lectern or table in front of you and must keep your notes in your hand.

Once you have decided where to be located, you can start thinking about exactly how you need to conduct yourself there.

The first rule is to *stand up straight*. You want to look smart and alert, not slovenly and slouching. Keeping your feet a little apart will keep you most comfortable, especially if you have to stand for any length of time.

The second rule is to *move*. Standing rigidly not only looks uncomfortable, it *is* uncomfortable. Worse, a static pose can engender a static delivery. Moving a little will:

- Facilitate a style that includes an appropriate amount of gestures

- ■ Help to maintain the audience's attention (they will have to make a little effort if you move around).

As with many of the techniques we are looking at, you can overdo movement. Too much and you may appear nervous, distracted, find yourself in the wrong place at the wrong moment. Balance is best, but some movement is essential – to you and the audience.

Look them in the eye

Think of some of the ways in which you do *not* want to be perceived – as anxious, nervous, incompetent, lacking credibility, uninterested in the audience (or even the task you are undertaking), rigid in your approach . . . you get the idea. The surest way to encourage such negative feelings is to avoid eye contact.

Good eye contact takes a little effort but will rapidly become a habit. It should be comprehensive, taking in the whole group (or all parts of a large audience), and it should be deliberate and seen to be intentional, though it should not become so regular in pattern as to suggest to the audience a routine rather than genuine interest and care.

Openness and care in this respect are very valuable. They increase audience focus and rapport, suggest confidence, allow greater assertiveness (where appropriate) and, coupled with the appropriate facial expression (whether that is a smile or a look of serious concentration), can make all the difference to the way a speaker is seen.

A helping hand

'What do I do with my hands?' is a common cry from the inexperienced speaker. It is all too easy to look awkward, and project a lack of confidence or authority which is best avoided. Thinking about your hands too much tends to compound any awkwardness. The best advice may be to forget them.

If that proves impossible, though, you might usefully cultivate a suitable resting position: one hand on a lectern or one by your side, for instance. Men should bear in mind that while one hand in the pocket can look acceptable, two always seems to look slovenly. For either sex, folded arms look defensive and reduce rapport.

The best approach is to give your hands *something to do*. For example:

- hold something: a pen, a reminder card, or a clipboard
- keep your hands and arms busy making gestures.

. . . and movement

Moderation in all things they say. And so it is with this aspect of physical animation: too much and it distracts. Too little and it – well, distracts and creates a feeling of uncertainty.

Two levels of gesture are important. First, simply relax, be comfortable (again, try not to think about it too much) and allow the spontaneous movements which accompany normal conversation to occur naturally.

Secondly, intentionally exaggerate selected movements to make a point. For example:

- pointing (to a slide or a member of the group)
- indicating size – for instance, as you say 'vast costs'
- counting, to match what you say: 'First, . . .'

Or, more dramatically:

- sweeping items (real or imaginary) off a table
- banging a fist down to emphasise a negative point.

What works best here *flows*: a comfortable resting position;

some regular natural movement; occasional intended and specific gestures; and back to resting.

And while all this is going on, you must also concentrate on how you sound.

Voice

Presentation does not need a special voice. Indeed, it would be difficult to sustain something artificial throughout a whole presentation. What is desirable, however, might best be described as an exaggeration of various voice elements.

■ *Speak up*: you need to be audible, but this should not involve strain. In a normal room (where there is no need for a microphone) you simply need to be conscious of addressing those furthest from you.

■ *Place the emphasis accurately*: this applies to both:

   — words: *place* the emphasis accurately/place the emphasis *accurately*

   — phrases: some sections are more important than others, and how you say them should make this clear (you can couple verbal emphasis with signposting: 'Now this is a key point, . . .'). In addition, the power of your voice affects emphasis. An extra firm tone suggests importance, but so can dropping the voice (think of the movies – the most menacing villain is often soft spoken)

■ *Pause regularly*: nervousness tends to make you omit pauses. It may take conscious effort (remember that what seems long to you, may only be a moment). A pause is very useful:

   — providing a moment for something to sink in

— focusing attention

— adding drama: the classic dramatic pause

— providing break points to separate different issues and, not least, giving you time to think, check progress or check timing.

- *Remember punctuation*: try not to draw breath where there is no clear pause, and remember to pause approximately when there should be, as it were, a comma or full stop

- *Choose your words carefully*: this links to both preparation and pace. If you are ill prepared and rushing along, words can become serviceable: '. . . this is important . . . ', rather than precise and appropriate: '. . . this can have a *catastrophic* effect . . .'. Detail is important here. Just one word can make a difference; or . . . *a powerful difference*.

- *Speak clearly*: to impress you must be heard and understood. Do not mumble. Exaggerate your clarity of speech for selected elements such as figures (effort here may also tend to slow you down a little, which may be no bad thing).

Remember too that the *pitch* of your voice conveys meaning in itself. A squeaky burst has none of the power you may have intended. *Inflection* can be used to add meaning as well. Are people clear that something is a question, for instance: can they *hear* the question mark?

There may seem to be a great many things to get your head round here, but practice will help make them become habits. The overall effect should be seamless and appear effortless. If your objectives are clear, you have a structure to follow and know which points you want to emphasise, then you will fall into a natural rhythm which adds pace, variety and emphasis as you go.

And finally . . .

There are two further ways of adding to the power, pace and variety of what you do: a little more drama, some humour, or both; but perhaps the first rule should be to use both carefully and not overdo either.

Let us take them in turn:

- *Adding drama*: this can involve a number of things and be as simple as a dramatic pause, but often involves exaggeration of voice and/or gesture. For example:

  — a simple phrase delivered with particular emphasis and/or the use of repetition (especially at the end of a sentence) '. . . so this is something we should not put up with – NOT FOR A SINGLE MOMENT!'

  — a really exaggerated gesture '. . . this is enough to make anyone *exhausted!*' (The presenter sits/collapses in the chair for a moment, before standing slowly and continuing in a measured manner)

  — something unashamedly theatrical. For example, I conduct courses on writing sales letters and will sometimes make a show of tearing something up and flinging it with great satisfaction into a waste bin to make the point that such correspondence must *earn* a reading, and the consequences if it fails to do so.

You may be able to think of other examples and will in any case want to find gestures and flourishes that fit with your style of presentation. Do not try something over-elaborate without care, practice or both – if it falls flat it will dilute the overall effect.

- *Adding humour*: there are, or should be, opportunities for light moments in many business presentations; but injecting them can be hazardous.

By saying 'Now here's a funny story . . .', you effectively alert people to the fact that a good laugh is imminent; if you then fail to provide one, you create an anticlimax and perhaps an awkward moment. More so if what is said is not simply not funny, but also inappropriate or embarrassing.

Be careful of anything where the difficulty of making it work is compounded by its nature. If something is in the nature of a tongue twister, if it demands a particular accent, or tends to prompt heckling and interruption, it may be better avoided.

Some things are always a safe bet. A quotation – 'As Gore Vidal said, "I like the way you always manage to state the obvious with a real sense of discovery", – may raise a smile (if not a laugh) and make a point. Even if it only accomplishes the latter, no great harm is done. Just the use of a less than serious phrase – likening a difficulty to 'nailing jam to the wall' – may not raise a laugh or even a smile (or be intended to), but can still act usefully as a slightly lighter moment. Again, this comes back to preparation, but it is also possible if you are feeling quick on your feet at a suitable moment.

Jokes have their place, of course. It would be a dull old world if no business presentation had room for an unashamed digression. But in my experience they work best if they do make a point (even if a somewhat contrived or distant one). And they should be tested. Try them out on a few people – not one polite one – to reduce any risk of failure.

Well, and appropriately, used humour is certainly useful. Apart from the immediate impact, it acts as dramatic punctuation.

5

A VISUAL ELEMENT

Perhaps the most important visual aid has already been mentioned: you. Factors, such as gestures and what was referred to in the last chapter as flourishes are part of this, as are your general manner and appearance.

More tangible forms of visual aid are also important. Such things as slides serve several roles, including:

- focusing attention within the group
- helping to change pace, add variety, etc
- giving visual support to a verbal explanation
- acting as signposts to where within the structure, the presentation has reached

They also help the presenter, providing reminders over and above speaker's notes, as to what comes next.

As always, be careful. Visual aids should *support* the message, not lead or take it over. Just because slides already exist or are easy to originate does not mean they will be right. You need to start by looking at the message, at what you are trying to do, and see what will help put it over and enhance. They may clarify a point that is difficult or impossible to describe, in the way a graph can illustrate a point which would be lost in a mass of figures. Or you may have a particular reason to use them; to help get a large amount of information over more quickly, perhaps.

The checklist* that follows deals, briefly, with the various options, and the two boxed paragraphs offer general guidance on visuals production, and some tips on using the ubiquitious OHP.

The most common forms of visual aid are:

- flipcharts
- OHPs (overhead projectors)
- table-top presenters
- fixed whiteboards
- handouts

The advantages and disadvantages of such visual displays can be compared as follows:

Flipcharts

Advantages

- no power source needed
- can be prepared beforehand
- can be adapted on the spot
- easy to see
- usually available in some form
- easy to write on
- colour can be used
- you can refer back to earlier sheets

Disadvantages

- expensive to prepare professionally
- very large and cumbersome to carry to an outside venue
- masking is difficult and can be untidy
- can sometimes look messy
- may not stand up to constant use

---

* This checklist, along with other material here, is adapted from the author's book *Running an Effective Training Session*, Gower Publishing.

In general, flipcharts are more useful as a group 'work pad' than as the basis of a presentation.

Overhead projectors

Advantages

- can be seen in even a bright room
- produce a large image
- masking is easily possible
- prepared slides easily carried
- can look professional
- commonly available
- can be used sitting down
- *aide mémoire* notes can be written on slide frame

with acetate roll attached:
- can also be used as a group work pad

Disadvantages

- need a power source
- can be noisy
- projection lens can block the view of the screen
- can break down
- limit to amount of information that can be legibly projected
- require a screen or a suitable wall
- tidy use requires discipline and experience

- not easy to write on without practice
- OHPs providing an acetate roll facility are usually bulky machines, though modern 'flat' OHPs are available with an acetate roll built in

---

OHPs are generally best used as the prepared base of a presentation, while the acetate roll is more useful as a 'work pad'.

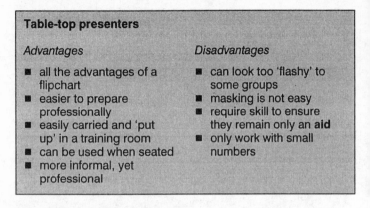

Table-top presenters

Advantages

- all the advantages of a flipchart
- easier to prepare professionally
- easily carried and 'put up' in a training room
- can be used when seated
- more informal, yet professional

Disadvantages

- can look too 'flashy' to some groups
- masking is not easy
- require skill to ensure they remain only an **aid**
- only work with small numbers

Generally, table-top presenters are an effective compromise, allowing pages to be prepared in advance and 'work pad' notes to be made. They also facilitate alterations.

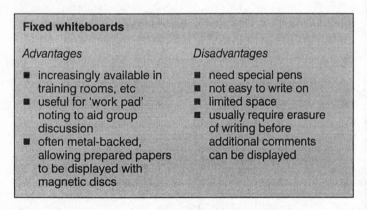

Fixed whiteboards

Advantages

- increasingly available in training rooms, etc
- useful for 'work pad' noting to aid group discussion
- often metal-backed, allowing prepared papers to be displayed with magnetic discs

Disadvantages

- need special pens
- not easy to write on
- limited space
- usually require erasure of writing before additional comments can be displayed

Useful only as a 'work pad' to highlight key points.

Handouts

Advantages	*Disadvantages*
■ can portray our professionalism	■ usually not personalised
■ highlighting of relevant points is possible	■ parts of content can be irrelevant or even counter-productive
■ can convey our technical expertise and give third party references	■ can detract from our verbal presentation

Generally useful as a support for the presentation argument, but it is not easy to condition and control the perception of the aid itself.

Increasingly, other aids – 35mm slides, video tapes, computer displays – are entering the presentational arena. Most can be excellent in their place; but may distance the audience from the presenter. Use them with caution, since the final impact will be dependent upon the participants' acceptance of the credibility of the speaker and the message, not on the supporting elements.

General principles of using visual aids

- Keep the content simple
- Restrict the amount of information and the number of words
    — use single words to give structure, headings, or short statements
    — avoid making it look cluttered or complicated
    — use a running logo (eg the main heading/topic on each slide)
- Use diagrams, graphs, etc where possible, rather than too many figures; and never read figures aloud without visual support

- Incorporate variety within the overall theme: eg with colour or variations of the form of aid used
- Emphasise the theme and structure: eg regularly use a single aid to recap the agenda or objectives
- Ensure that the content of the visual aid matches the words
- Make sure content is necessary and relevant
- Ensure everything is visible. Ask yourself: is it clear? will it work in this room? does it suit the equipment? (Well-chosen colours, and the right sized typeface help here)
- Ensure the layout emphasises the meaning you want (and not some minor detail)
- Pick the right aid for the right purpose (see list).

Using an OHP (overhead projector)

Care should be taken in using an overhead projector. They appear simple, but present inherent hazards to the unwary. The following hints may well be useful:

- Make sure the electric flex is out of the way (or taped to the floor)
- Make sure it works before you start using it with the group (this goes for the second bulb – and a spare, even – and the roll of acetate film if you are using one)
- Make sure it is positioned where you want it; within reach, and giving you room to move and with space alongside for papers. (Note that it may need to be in a slightly different place for left/right-handed people – a potential hazard for some team presentations)
- Stand back and to one side of it: be sure not to obscure anyone's view of the screen
- Having made sure the picture is in focus, look at the machine and not the screen
- Only use slides that have sufficiently large typefaces or

images and, if you plan to write on acetate, check how large your handwriting needs to be

- Switch off when changing slides; it looks more professional than the jumbled image that appears otherwise

- If you want to project the image on a slide progressively you can cover the bottom part of the image with a sheet of paper; this allows you to see the whole image through it even though it won't be projected.

- Use an acetate roll (fitted running from the back to the front of the machine) if you are handwriting your projections, as this minimises the amount of acetate used (it is expensive) and obviates the need to keep changing loose sheets

- Remember that when something new is shown, all attention is, at least momentarily, focused on it – pause, or what you say may be missed

- It may be useful to add emphasis by highlighting certain things on the slides as you go through them; if you slip the slide *under* the acetate roll you can do this without adjustment and without marking the slide

- Similarly, two slides shown together can add information (or you can use overlays attached to the slide and folded across). Alternatively, the second slide may have minimal information on it, with such things as a talk title, session heading, or company logo remaining in view on one as others are shown by being placed over it

- If you want to point something out, this is most easily done by laying a small pointer (or pencil) on the projector.

Whatever you use, remember to talk to the group not to the visual aid. Looking at the screen too much when an OHP is used is a common fault. Make sure visuals are visible (do not get in the way yourself), explain them or their purpose as necessary, mention whether or not they will get a paper copy of them and stop them distracting the audience by removing them as soon as you are finished with them.

Beware gremlins

It is axiomatic that if something can go wrong it will; and nowhere is this more true than with equipment.

The moral: check, check and check again. Everything – from the spare OHP bulb (do not even think about using an old machine with only one bulb) to which way up 35mm slides are going to be, and even whether the pens for the flipchart still work – is worth checking.

Always double check anything with which you are unfamiliar, especially if what you do is going to be significantly dependent on it. And remember that while the sophistication of equipment increases all the time (a laptop computer linked to an OHP allows first class, coloured graphics to be projected at the touch of a button), so too do the number of things that can go wrong.

It is worth considering a contingency plan: what do you do if disaster does strike? You have been warned.

Anything and everything

Finally, be inventive. Practically anything can act as a visual aid, from another person (carefully briefed to play their part) to an exhibit. In a business presentation, exhibits may be obvious items: products, samples, posters, etc; or maybe something totally unexpected.

There are venues whose proud boast is that they have the facilities to allow you to say 'What we need now is some really heavyweight support', as the baby elephant actually walks across the platform behind you.

This may be a little far-fetched but like all the skills of presentation, while the basics give you a sound foundation, you can always benefit from a little imagination.